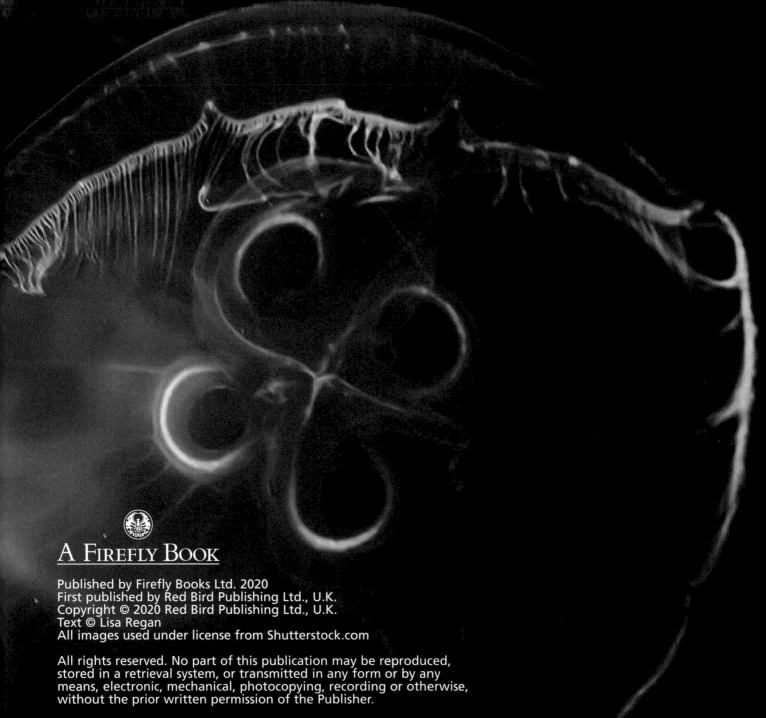

A FIREFLY BOOK

Published by Firefly Books Ltd. 2020
First published by Red Bird Publishing Ltd., U.K.
Copyright © 2020 Red Bird Publishing Ltd., U.K.
Text © Lisa Regan
All images used under license from Shutterstock.com

First printing

Library of Congress Control Number: 2020934073

Library and Archives Canada Cataloguing in Publication
Title: Nature at night : amazing creatures that light up / Lisa Regan.
Names: Regan, Lisa, 1971- author.
Identifiers: Canadiana 20200199595 | ISBN 9780228102557 (hardcover) |
ISBN 9780228102540 (softcover)
Subjects: LCSH: Bioluminescence—Juvenile literature. | LCSH:
Biofluorescence—Juvenile literature. |
   LCSH: Animal behavior—Juvenile literature.
Classification: LCC QH641 .R44 2020 | DDC j572/.4358—dc23

Published in Canada by
Firefly Books Ltd.
50 Staples Avenue, Unit 1
Richmond Hill, Ontario
L4B 0A7

Published in the United States by
Firefly Books (U.S.) Inc.
P.O. Box 1338, Ellicott Station
Buffalo, New York
14205

Printed in China

Nature at Night

Written by Lisa Regan

FIREFLY BOOKS

Imagine a place where fish light up, jellyfish look like fireworks, and mushrooms glow in the dark. Next, turn the pages to find that it's real! Scientists now know of more and more organisms that light up in the darkness, on land and in the water. Explore these fascinating creations for yourself with a book full of glowing wonders of the world!

Contents

When you see a ☆, hold the book under a light source for thirty seconds. Then turn off the lights to see the pages glow!

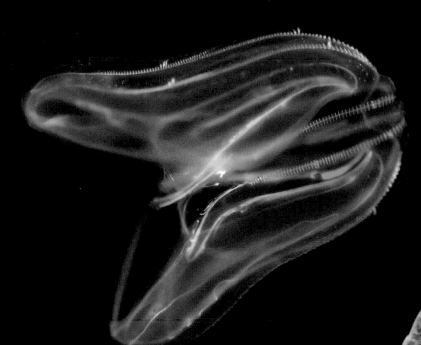

Bioluminescence

A creature or living thing that is bioluminescent (say it: by-oh-loo-min-ess-unt) can make light in its own body. A combination of chemicals causes a reaction that converts chemical energy into light, in the same way that a glow stick glows when you crack it.

Biofluorescence

Biofluorescent (say it: by-oh-fluh-ress-unt) creatures and organisms cannot make their own light. Instead, they soak up natural light and send it back out again, usually with a little less energy so it changes shade to green, orange or red.

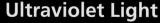

Ultraviolet Light

There are some light waves that humans cannot see. Many other living things, including birds, insects, fish, and some mammals, can see a range of light that we cannot. They use ultraviolet patterns and markings to help them find food or protect them from predators. People can see this UV glow using a black light source.

*Look for the **highlighted** words in the glossary at the back of the book.*

Dinoflagellate

A kind of **bioluminescence** known as sea sparkle has been recorded by sailors for centuries. It is caused when tiny single-celled **plankton**, known as dinoflagellates (say it: dy-noh-fla-juh-layts) are agitated, for example by a boat or by waves. This triggers a **chemical reaction** within the creatures.

Scientists believe that this beautiful blue glow is used as a kind of burglar alarm. It attracts bigger creatures that will frighten off anything that is a threat to the dinoflagellates themselves.

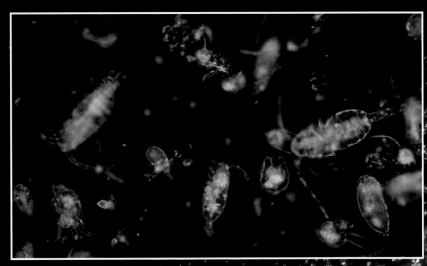

The largest dinoflagellates are the size of a grain of rice.

The motion of the waves creates sea sparkle in Samut Sakhon Province in Thailand.

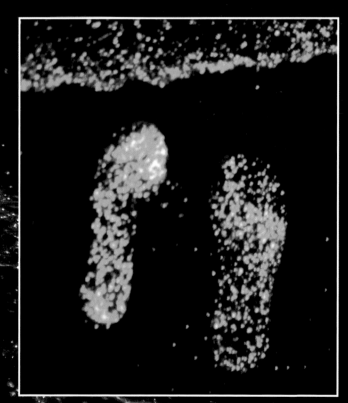

Walking in the water causes the creatures to bioluminesce where they are disturbed.

Glowworms

These insects are found only in New Zealand and Australia and, although they are called glowworms, they are actually a type of gnat (say it: nat). In their young, wingless stage they produce bioluminescent light to attract their **prey**.

These young **larvae** (say it: lar-vee) shelter in caves and make long silken threads to hang down from the cave roof as traps. Each thread has drops of **mucus**, sometimes poisonous, to catch passing moths and flies. A hungry glowworm is brighter than one that has eaten.

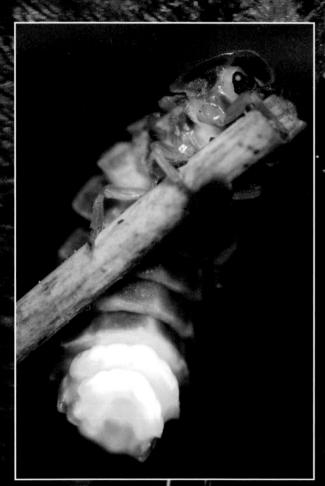

The adults make bioluminescent lights to attract a mate.

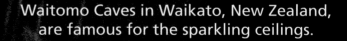

Waitomo Caves in Waikato, New Zealand, are famous for the sparkling ceilings.

Each larva makes up to seventy long threads.

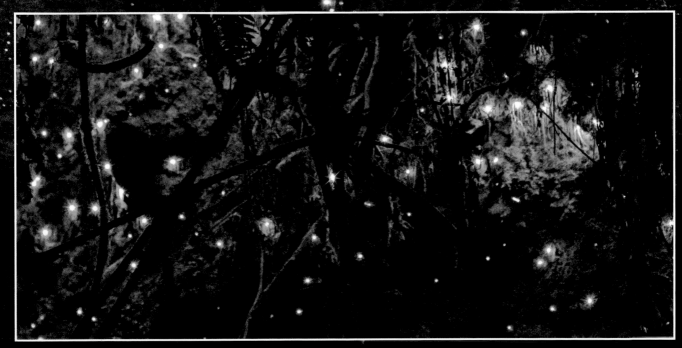

A colony of adult glowworms lights up their forest home at night.

Foxfire Fungi

There are around 70 types of bioluminescent mushrooms, and their brightness can vary depending on the species. Some of the Australian ones glow intensely, while North American ones have a dimmer light. The mushrooms are used to make glow-in-the-dark face paint in some places!

This Australian mushroom is called ghost fungus.

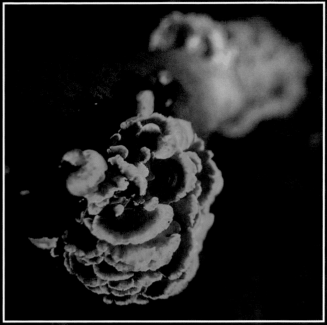

This fungus is nicknamed "bitter oyster" and grows in many countries.

Sometimes described as fairy fire, it is thought that foxfire mushrooms glow to attract insects which spread the mushroom **spores** around the forest. However some types of **fungus** have glowing stems, probably to stop them being eaten.

Click Beetle

This beetle gets its name from the noise it makes when it snaps the front sections of its body together. They make this loud click to scare off **predators**, or to flip themselves onto their feet if they get tipped onto their back by accident.

Certain click beetles have bioluminescent dots on their body which helps to warn their enemies not to eat them. They cannot flash these lights but they can make them brighter if a **predator** comes close.

Chameleon

Check out a chameleon under black or **ultraviolet** light, and you will see its head glowing! Scientists have only recently discovered that this glow comes from their skull. The bones fluoresce and re-emit light back through the skin to form amazing patterns.

Biofluorescence is rare in creatures that live on land.

Some types of chameleon have glowing bumps known as tubercles (say it: to-berkulz) all along their body. The skin over the bones is thin enough to allow light through, charging up the fluorescent bumps and turning the re-emitted light blue.

Crocodiles

Crocodiles, alligators and caimans are all related but live in different parts of the world. They are large reptiles with a long snout and sharp teeth for catching fish and other animals. Each of them has a special layer at the back of their eyes that makes them shine in the darkness.

The layer is called the tapetum (say it: tah-pet-um) and it reflects back light that shines on the animal's eyes. The reflection can be red, orange, pink, yellow or white. The tapetum is present in all kinds of creatures and it helps them to see better at night.

This is an American alligator at sunset.

The caiman is found from Mexico down to South America.

The Nile crocodile's eyes are green in the daytime.

Hawksbill Sea Turtle

Hawksbill turtles are found mostly in the tropics, and their numbers have dropped so much and so quickly that they are a critically endangered species. Scientists have recently discovered that their shells glow red and green with **biofluorescence**.

The green glow is from the turtle's shell, but the red glow comes both from the turtle itself and from a coating of **algae** (say it: al-gee or al-jee) on its back. It could be a form of camouflage, helping the turtle to blend in with biofluorescent coral at night.

Now scientists want to study other turtles to see if they are fluorescent too.

Jellyfish

Jellyfish are an excellent example of the sea creatures that typically use **bioluminescence**, for several reasons. They use the light to attract a **mate**, to draw in **prey**, and to scare off any predators.

Jellyfish are mostly made up of water and do not have a brain. Actually, they don't have many body parts at all: no blood, no bones, no heart, and no lungs!

Many jellyfish don't swim but float in ocean currents.

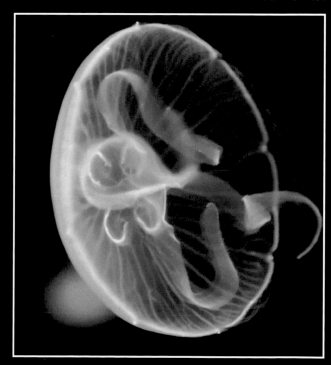

Fimbriated Moray Eel

This long, skinny fish is another underwater animal that absorbs light and beams it back out as a different, brightly glowing shade. This night-time signal might help the eels to find a **mate** during a full moon, when the moon's blue light is at its brightest.

Two types of false moray eel also glow in an amazing way. Eels are the only fish known to fluoresce inside AND out, making every part of them glow green: not only the skin but also their muscles and organs.

Fimbriated moray eels are also known as spot-face morays or darkspotted morays.

A moray eel has a good sense of smell, with nostrils that poke up from its snout.

Flashlight Fish

The bean-shaped light underneath this fish's eyes is made by bioluminescent **bacteria**. They live in pockets below the eye socket.

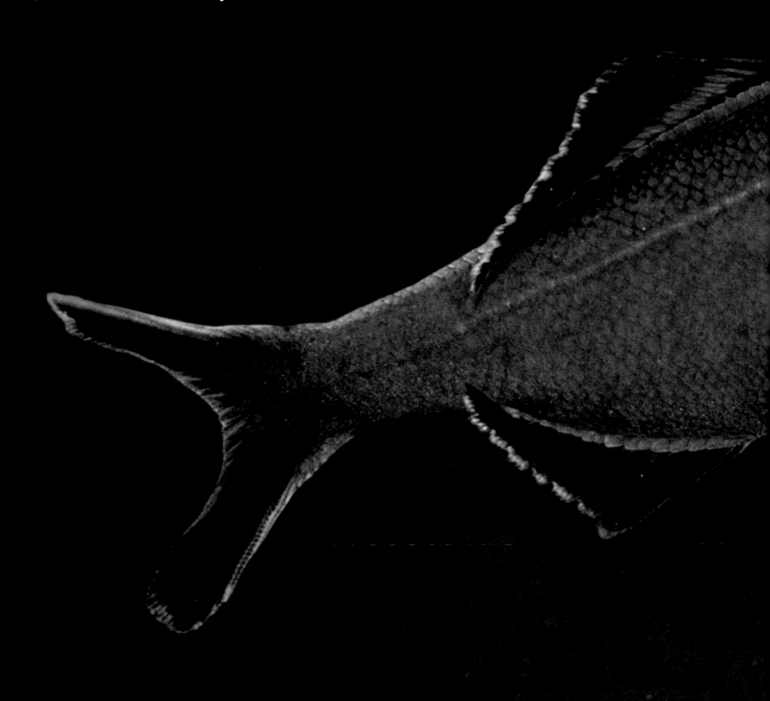

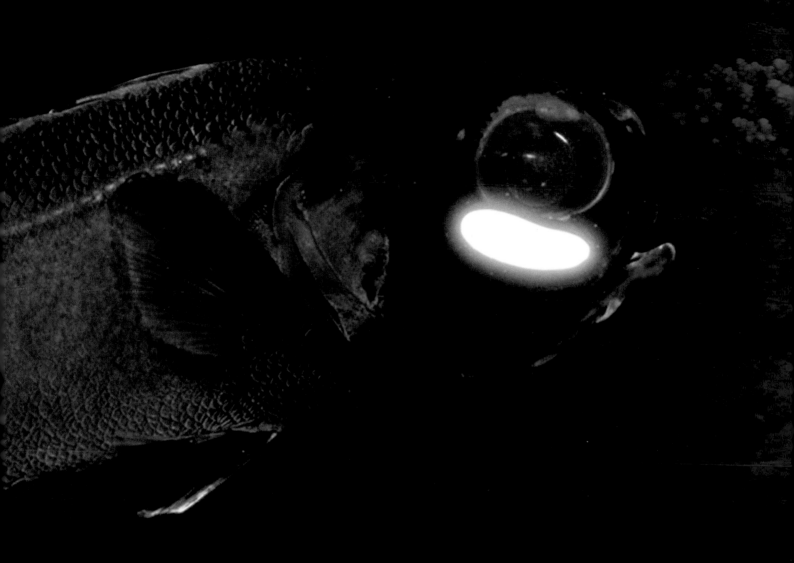

The bacteria make the light all the time but the fish can produce a flashing effect by blinking. The fish use these flashes to send messages to each other.

The fish blink at different intervals, sometimes just twice a minute but up to once every second. The flashes have been used by sailors to help guide them around coral reefs at night-time.

Lizardfish

Many fluorescent fish are hard to see in ordinary white light. Lots of them, like this lizardfish, are camouflaged with patterned skin that looks like their surroundings. However, shine a blue or black light on them, and their neon glow makes them instantly stand out from the background.

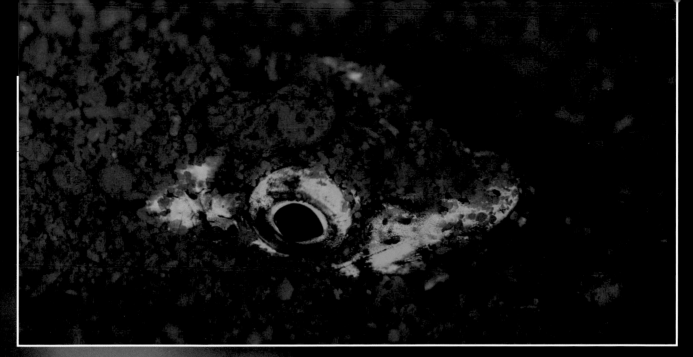

Lizardfish often bury themselves in the sand on the ocean floor.

Different lizardfishes have different fluorescent markings. They can see each other and use the markings to help them find members of the same species.

Eye-Flash Squid

This creature is tiny—shorter than your thumb—but quite amazing. It gets its name from lights underneath its eyes, but it also has around 550 tiny bioluminescent dots all over its body. These flash in different patterns to thoroughly confuse its enemies.

Not only can it flash, it can also change its lights from blue to green and back again. It uses these different colors to hide in moonlight or against different levels of lighting.

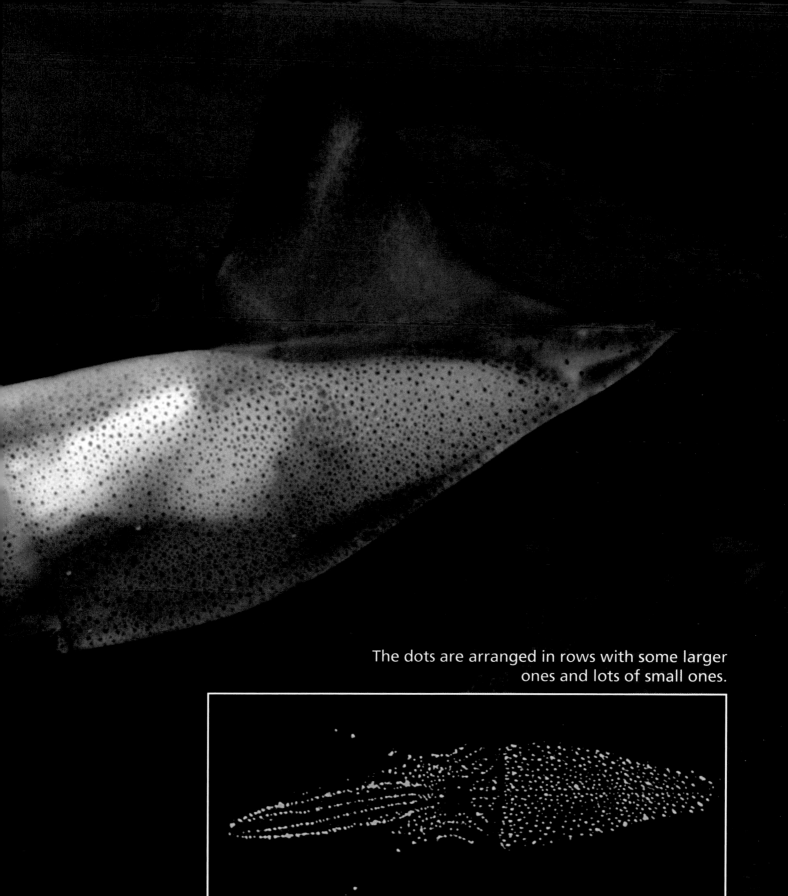

The dots are arranged in rows with some larger ones and lots of small ones.

Decapod Shrimp

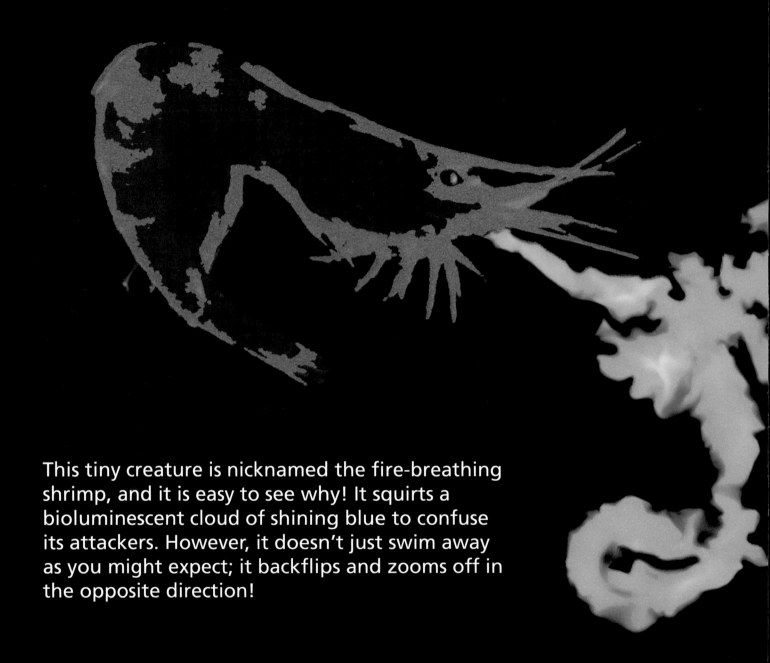

This tiny creature is nicknamed the fire-breathing shrimp, and it is easy to see why! It squirts a bioluminescent cloud of shining blue to confuse its attackers. However, it doesn't just swim away as you might expect; it backflips and zooms off in the opposite direction!

The shrimp stores one of the substances needed for this chemical reaction inside its body. When it is squirted into the water, it reacts with the oxygen there to produce the burst of **bioluminescence**.

Polka Dot Tree Frog

This small forest-dwelling frog was the first amphibian (say it: am-fib-ee-yun) found to have fluorescent qualities. It lives in South America and grows to around 3 cm (1 in) long.

The frog glows in natural light such as twilight and moonlight.

In the daylight, the frog's skin appears pale green with white, yellow, or red spots, and a stripe running down its sides. By night, it looks more reddish. Under black light, however, it gives off a bright green fluorescence.

The frog produces special fluorescent secretions that make its skin glow. Scientists only discovered this by accident when they were doing other studies that needed UV lights.

Swallowtail Butterfly

All butterflies have scales on their wings and it is these scales that give them their patterns and colors. They will often have completely different markings on the top side and the underside.

These scales interfere with the light, and sections of the wings of the African swallowtail are extra special. They filter out certain wavelengths and reflect waves in the **ultraviolet** range, making the butterfly's wings shine with fluorescent blue and green light.

The swallowtail is a large butterfly with a wingspan of up to 9.5 cm (3.7 in).

Scorpion

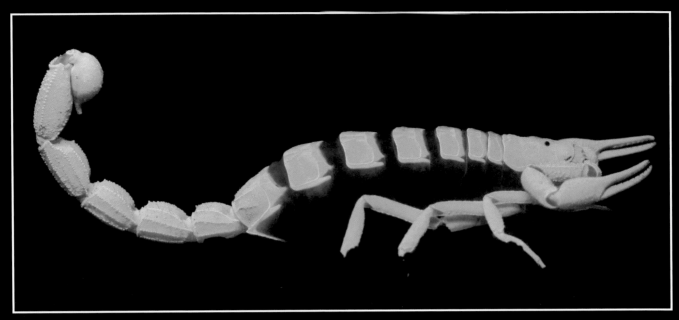

Scientists first discovered that scorpions glow in 1954.

Scorpions are arachnids (say it: uh-rak-nidz) with a hard exoskeleton on the outside and a venomous stinger on the end of their tail. A substance in their outer layer makes them glow under **ultraviolet** light, or even in the light of the moon.

This substance, called hyaline (say it: hee-uh-lin or hy-uh-lin) has even been found in fossils that are millions of years old. It still fluoresces, too! Scientists have discovered that scorpions don't glow when they have shed their old exoskeleton. They do this to grow into a new, bigger one, which glows once it becomes hard.

One of nature's most spectacular sights is a night-time light show in the sky, known as the aurora (say it: or-or-uh). It appears above the North and South Poles and can shine green and sometimes red and blue.

The lights are caused by charged particles from the Sun which blow toward the Earth's magnetic poles. As they enter the atmosphere they crash into other particles and release energy in the form of light.

They are commonly known as the Northern Lights and the Southern Lights.

Firefly

Fireflies are sometimes known as lightning bugs.

38

Fireflies are actually a type of beetle, and they make their own "cold light" using **bioluminescence**. It is produced by chemicals in their lower body, and can be green, yellow, or sometimes pink.

Whole colonies of fireflies light up at dusk and flash their lights on and off, probably to attract a **mate**. Each firefly is only around the size of a fingernail, but they gather in their hundreds or thousands to light up the woods and forests.

Octopus

All octopuses have eight arms or tentacles, but this glowing sucker octopus looks a little different. Its arms are not all the same length; the longest one grows to around 35 cm (14 in).

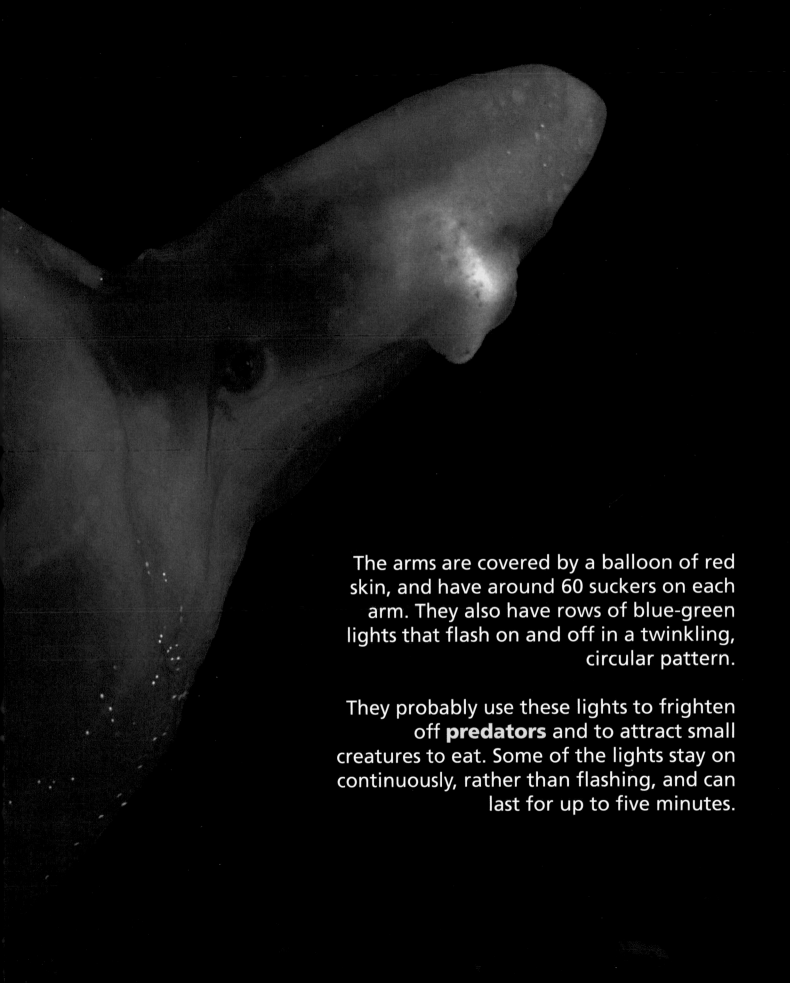

The arms are covered by a balloon of red skin, and have around 60 suckers on each arm. They also have rows of blue-green lights that flash on and off in a twinkling, circular pattern.

They probably use these lights to frighten off **predators** and to attract small creatures to eat. Some of the lights stay on continuously, rather than flashing, and can last for up to five minutes.

41

Atolla Jellyfish

Like many deep-sea creatures, this one has a red body. This makes it almost invisible to other animals in the deep waters, beyond the reach of sunlight. It has around 20 tentacles plus one that is much longer than the others, which is used for breeding and catching food.

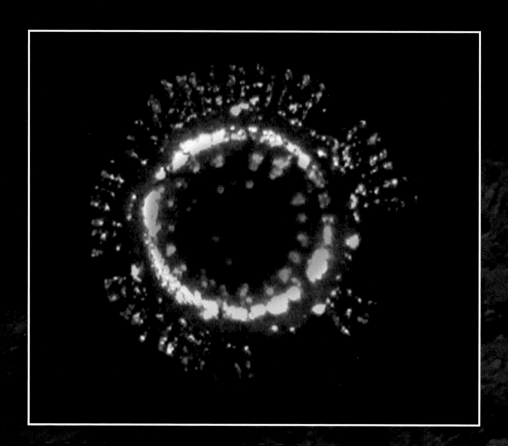

The Atolla jellyfish uses its **bioluminescence** to protect itself. If under attack, it flashes to attract other creatures which will approach and scare away (or even eat) the Atolla's attacker.

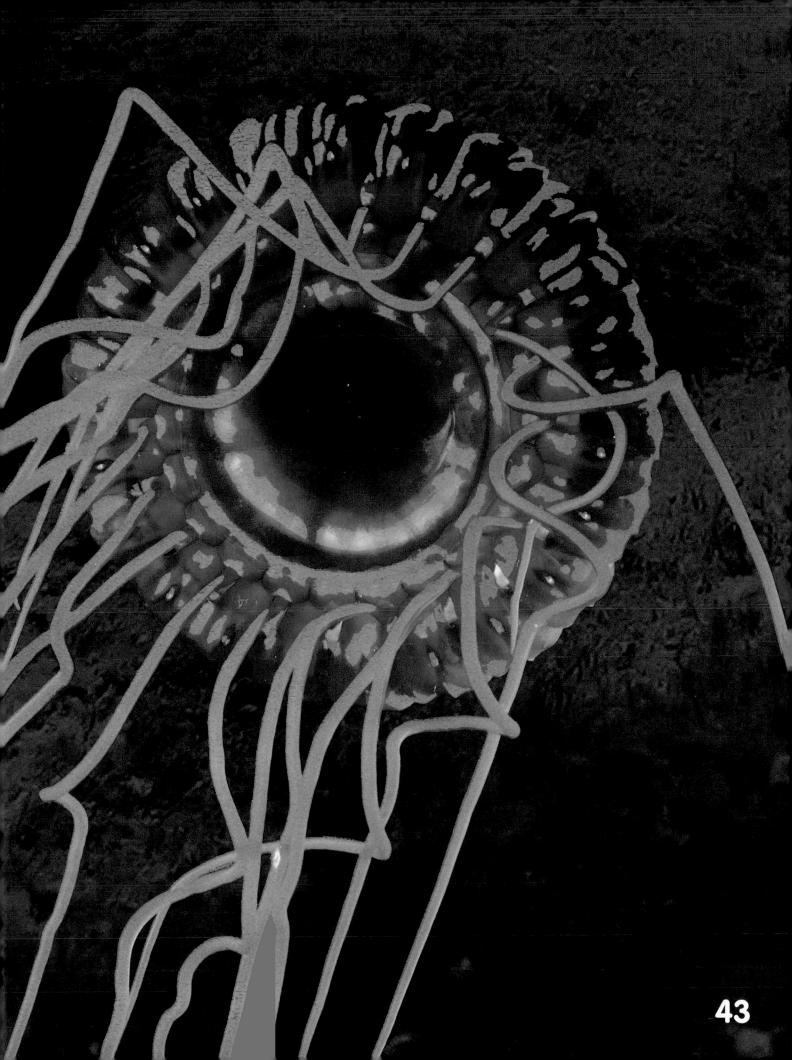

Lanternfish

Lanternfish have a line of **photopores** (say it: foh-toh-porz) down each side of their body that make light. They probably use these lights to attract a **mate**, deep down in the dark ocean waters that they live in.

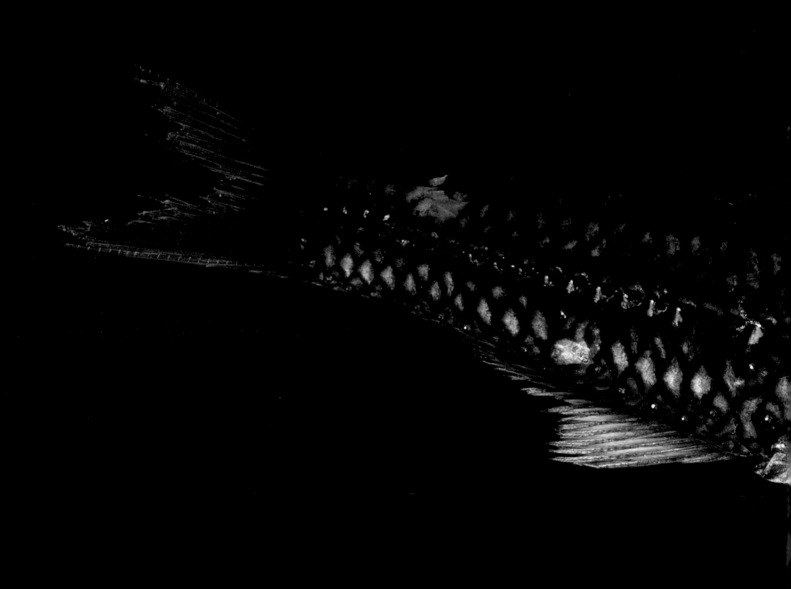

The fish spend the daytime in the depths and then swim up toward the surface at night to feed on **plankton**. Their lights may help them stay in shoals with similar fish, as different species of lanternfish have different patterns or colors, ranging from pale blue and green to yellow.

Like all stingrays, this fish has a pointed tail with a venomous spike on it. The yellow stingray's sting can be painful but is not dangerous to humans. This creature is a small ray, growing to only around 36 cm (14 in) across and 70 cm (28 in) long. It can alter its color to match its surroundings and completely blend in with the sea floor. It is biofluorescent, and when seen under a black light it glows with a distinctive pattern of green markings.

Puffin

This seabird's beak is one of its most distinctive features, but it hides a fluorescent secret! Puffins can see light wavelengths that humans cannot, and scientists believe that birds can see the fluorescent markings even in ordinary daylight. It may help them to identify each other, or to attract a **mate**. And picture this: scientists wanting to test the puffins had special sunglasses made to protect the birds' eyes from the UV light!

Glossary

algae	a type of simple water plant such as seaweed
bacteria	tiny living things that are too small to see
biofluorescence	the ability to absorb blue light and re-emit it as a different color
bioluminescence	the ability of some creatures to produce their own light
chemical reaction	making a new substance from two or more substances; light or heat can be given off during the reaction
dusk	the time when day turns into night
fungus (plural: fungi)	a class of living things that is neither animal nor plant, but feeds on decomposing material
larva (plural = larvae)	an insect after it hatches from an egg but before it becomes an adult; also known as "grub"
mate	a partner for producing babies
mucus	a slimy substance produced by living things
organism	a living thing such as an animal, plant, fungus, or bacteria
photophores	spots on a creature's body that give off light
plankton	a mixture of tiny plants and animals that float in the ocean
predator	an animal that hunts other creatures for food
prey	an animal that is hunted and eaten by other creatures
spores	tiny cells given off by fungi to spread and grow new fungi
ultraviolet	waves of light that are shorter than visible rays, but which can still be seen by some animals